Mental Toughness
Understanding the Game of Life

DR. TIMOTHY S. WAKEFIELD

www.developingmentaltoughness.com

authorHOUSE®

AuthorHouse™
1663 Liberty Drive, Suite 200
Bloomington, IN 47403
www.authorhouse.com
Phone: 1-800-839-8640

First published by AuthorHouse 12/11/2008

ISBN: 978-1-4389-0464-1 (sc)

Printed in the United States of America
Bloomington, Indiana

This book is printed on acid-free paper.

Introduction

I have three boys. Initially, I wrote this to read to our children when they graduated from high school. As I finished writing this and shared this with our first son, friends and family thought this was information that many could learn from, including themselves. I was encouraged to publish this, so I did. I started this letter by giving our first son some "stuff" that I wanted him to have to lead his life in the future.

This "stuff" consisted of:

1. A map of USA and Canada—to assist him in planning his trips and when he is lost.
2. A Bible—to assist him when he is planning his life and when he is lost in life.
3. Audio books to listen to while traveling to and from college: The purpose of these audio books is to hear the views of others on how to achieve goals and dreams. Much of this information he has heard in the past. It is good to have the views of others. This will help to show him how to have the richest, most fulfilling life possible. Examples of these audio books:
    Think and Grow Rich
    As a Man Thinketh
    The Richest Man in Babylon
    How to Win Friends and Influence People
4. A "letter of gratification" I had written explaining to him how proud of him I am, emphasizing his strengths and future opportunities.

It took me over two years to write this for our boys. I thought of this letter/book to our boys as I was driving down the road, taking our children from practice to practice and game to game. After we got past "how was your day?" there were many times with periods of awkward silence. Neither one of us knew what to talk about. Periodically, a common news story would come up about a school shooting, an abduction, an abuse victim, or a national catastrophe. I knew in my heart that if I had conversations about these "negative things" it would attract more "negative things" to their life. I had to stop that. I still had a problem. I did not know what to talk about during these times of awkward silence. This was a very difficult time for me. I had experience with public speaking in front of hundreds of people, and I did not know what to talk about to my ten-year-old son. What was wrong with me? I felt foolish. So I stepped back and analyzed my life and the lives of the successful people around me. I decided to teach my children about the things that it took me forty-plus years of listening to my family, taking seminars, reading books, listening to tapes/CDs, etc., to learn to achieve success and happiness. I thought to myself that there were hundreds of self-help books, CDs, DVDs, and seminars out there for adults. Why not teach this to kids and young adults? So I started talking to our children about positive life experiences and a way to lead a positive, happy, successful, and productive life. I would start conversations by asking them questions or talking about things like:

> Tell me what you know about being honest.
> Do you know what integrity is?
> Do you know what perseverance is?
> Do you know what it means to "master the things that do not take talent"?
> What do you value in yourself and in others? Things like honesty, respect, politeness, etc.
> What do you think you are great at?
> What would you like to be better at?
> What does respect mean to you?
> What are manners, and why do you think we should use them?
> Etc.

Following their response I would write up a paragraph about the subject and place it in a file. That is how this book began. This is a book to have as a personal reference and to read many times throughout your life, especially when times are tough. I still read this a couple times per year—just to remind me of the GOOD STUFF in the world!

As I wrote this I realized it was not just for kids and young people but easy concepts for ALL to follow and build a positive, happy, successful, and productive life.

Good luck, and enjoy the concepts of this book. Take the information for what it is worth. Understand the concepts, apply them to your life, and do not "read between the lines." I wrote this with the "KISS" principal in mind. Keep It Short and Simple. I wrote this to assist us in looking at all the positive in the world, the great opportunities we all have. This book, most of all, will help us gain control of our lives. I read this entire book out loud to our oldest son when he graduated from high school. It took me ninety minutes. It was one of the best ninety minutes I have ever spent.

Please enjoy *Mental Toughness: Understanding the Game of Life.*

Table of Contents

Three Things that Can Change Your Life in a Fraction of a Second

The three things that can change your life in a fraction of a second are:

1. Sex
2. Drugs
3. Alcohol

As you get older you may experiment with sex. In most schools there are sex education classes. With these classes you have been taught how to protect yourself and your partner; please be careful with sexual activity. A sexually transmitted disease or a pregnancy can change your life, your entire life. Please be open with your partner and communicate about sexual activity. Discussing sexual activity can be embarrassing, but it is an important part of life. Sexual activity is an important part of a relationship for both the male and the female. Make sure you communicate about your sexual relationship and sexual activity and understand each of your likes and dislikes. Remember to use the appropriate forms of contraception (condoms, the pill, etc). Sexual activity can change the outcome of your entire life. I encourage you to discuss sexual activity with a parent, relative, or close adult before engaging in sexual activity. The more you know and understand, the less chance of making a mistake that could affect your entire life. Please be careful with sexual activity.

If you have not yet been exposed to drugs in high school, you may be in college, at work, or in the future. There is absolutely no win to taking drugs. You can risk everything you have worked for your entire life by trying drugs just once. It is not worth the risk to your body, your character, or your reputation. There is no win with taking drugs.

You may have seen adults drink alcohol since you have been young. Once you are of legal drinking age, alcohol consumption can be OK as long as you control the amount of alcohol you consume and NOT have the alcohol control you. Alcohol can "cloud your judgment" and can lead you into making poor choices. Always be in control of your choices. People can become dependant on alcohol; this can be bad and destroy your health and relationships with others. Be careful with your consumption of alcohol. Be careful with the amount of the consumption and the frequency of the consumption, if you choose to consume.

Male/Female Relationships

In general, males and females have different needs.
Understand that most *males* have to be physical (touching) before becoming emotional (expressing feelings verbally).
Understand that most *females* have to become emotional (expressing feelings verbally) before becoming physical (touching).

This means that to have a good relationship with your wife or girlfriend you have to let them talk, and you must just listen whether you agree or not. This is quite difficult for me and most men. Understand that females do not want **you** to solve their problems; they just want you to listen. They are not asking for your opinion and, quite frankly, don't want your guidance on how to think. They want to think through it themselves. Females, generally, do that with their mouth.

Understand that it is difficult for most men to sit, listen, and ask questions about the subject, and NOT give solutions until asked. In order to have a good healthy relationship with most females you must: listen—not talk; ask questions—not give answers; and let them work through their own issues and concerns. When females want your help, they will ask for it. If what they want is unclear to you, then ask them, "Are you asking me to help you with a solution, or do you want me to listen and help you talk through this?"

In general, females like to be listened to, told they are beautiful, smart, a great mother, cook, wife, etc. Females like to *assume* that males know what they want/think. Males don't take hints well. Make sure you tell your significant other to ask for what she wants and do not *assume* you will know by the hints that she thinks she has given you. Females like to be surprised with little things, flowers, candy, etc. They like to know that they are thought about throughout your day.

Many males like to feel they are the primary provider for the family. They like to feel like the "King of Their Castle." Males like to feel they are the "hunter-gatherers" for the family. Males like to feel they "bring home the bacon." Males like to have their hands held when walking down the road, their shoulders rubbed when sitting at home, and in general like to be quiet when at home. Men are generally thinkers, not talkers. Males are generally "problem solvers." So it helps males to "think" about their problems and come up with a "solution" to discuss. It helps females to "talk" about their "problems"; they may never come up with a solution, but they feel better for having talked about it.

As you can see from the paragraphs above, these two approaches to "problem solving" can cause conflict between males and females. This may cause conflict *if* the way males and females think is not understood by both the male and the female in every relationship. This may be a boyfriend/girlfriend, husband/wife, employer/employee, etc. Understand that this is important in all relationships between members of the opposite sex.

If you are male, to have a good relationship with your wife, girlfriend, etc. (or any other female besides your mother), you need to be patient, to listen to her, and to ask questions about the things she does, showing interest and concern. Do not give solutions unless asked for.

If you are female, to have a good relationship with your husband, boyfriend, etc., do not assume your hints are being taken; tell them what you want. Be patient when at home. Do not assume that when he is quiet that he is mad; he may be just thinking. Let him talk about ideas, concepts, and solutions. It does not mean he is going to run out and do them. Most likely he is talking through the multitude of solutions to his issue.

Understanding both sides of the male–female relationship will help both to understand each other's needs.

Establish Your "Core Values"

Core values are your morals. Your core values are what you value and what you think is ethical. These are qualities such as honesty, faith, dedication, integrity, hard work, self-discipline, etc. Write down your seven to ten most important human qualities. You must take your time with this. It may take ten to fifteen minutes to drill down and get the answers. (You may add others as the days, months, and years go by.)

1.

2.

3.

4.

5.

6.

7.

8.

9.

10.

This list is some of your core values. When finding a girlfriend, wife, business partner, etc., it is most important that you both have the same core values and interests. You will/may be spending the rest of your life together. Make sure you choose your partners wisely.

Your future spouse, business partners, etc., must have these same or similar values in order for that relationship to last and be a success. These are critical for developing a long-term relationship.

Mental Law of Success

That which we can conceive of, believe in, and confidently expect of ourselves must become our experience. The inside of your head determines the outside of your life. Our thoughts and feelings attract our life to us. The way we look at the world is the way the people of the world look back at us. You are how you think. If we think positive thoughts, we will have a positive life. If we think negative thoughts, we will have a negative life. If we are critical of ourselves and other people, we will attract more of what we are critical of. If we say something negative about someone else, it will come back to haunt us. Garbage in—garbage out. Greatness in—greatness out. We are right now where our mind has been in the past. By managing our mind we can change its effect. If you think something won't work, it won't. You cannot do something you think you cannot. Your thoughts and beliefs control your life. What you think and believe is what you will get out of life. Whether you think you can or you can't—you are correct. Understand that your thoughts must be backed up by physical action in order to succeed. This is the physical law of success. Control your mind, add physical action, and you will control your success. This is commonly called "mental toughness." Mental toughness allows you to keep focused and not be distracted by outside influences that may take you off course. You have control over the way you think. The way you think will control your destiny. If you perform "stinkin' thinkin'," you will be "stinkin'." If you choose to think like a "champion," you will become a "champion." It is truly up to you. Your thoughts control your destiny, and you control your thoughts. Positive thinking is the "hope" that you can move mountains. Positive "believing" is the same hope but with a reason for believing you can do it. Think great thoughts and believe that you can do it.

Physical Law of Success

The Physical Law of Success states that the more physical energy you put into something, the more you will get out of it. You are as good right now as you've really wanted to be in the past. Nothing can prevent you from having what you sincerely desire as long as you are willing to put out the physical effort to attain it.

If you want to be stronger, work on your strength.
If you want to be faster, work on your speed.
If you want to be better at a skill, work on that skill.
If you want to be smarter, study more.
If you want others to respect you, respect others.
If you want others to be polite to you, be polite to others.
If you want a friend, be a friend.
No good effort is ever wasted.

The harder you work, the harder it becomes for others to defeat you.
The harder you work, the harder it is for you to surrender.
The harder you work, the luckier you get.
Luck is when preparation meets opportunity.
Work hard, and people will call you "lucky."

When a person receives an award, college scholarship, or special recognition, many people call him/her "lucky."

The best compliment you can get is if a person calls you "lucky." ***You create your own luck.*** The people that call you "lucky" were not there and do not see the sacrifice that you have made to create your "luck." People were "sleeping in" when you were waking up at 5:20 a.m., picking up younger athletes and in the weight room by 6:00 a.m., and working hard until 7:30 a.m. Fellow athletes were leaving at the end of practice when you were staying an extra thirty to forty-five minutes to work on a skill. Fellow athletes were staying home, watching TV, and playing video games when you were going to camps, working on skills in your backyard, analyzing films, and going to the field or gym to train more. These people were not there when you got home at 10:00 p.m., stayed up until midnight studying for a test, and still picked up additional athletes and made it to the weight room by 6:00 a.m. These people were not there when you missed the dance or the party with your friends. These people were not there when people told you that you were too slow, you were too small, you were too weak, or you were not mentally tough enough to play.

These people were not there to see the dedication, sacrifices, and heartaches that you went through to take advantage of your opportunities. Luck is when preparation meets opportunity. You have prepared, and now people call you "lucky." Do not be embarrassed by, belittle, or avoid recognition for your success. Be proud of your accomplishments but not arrogant. When people point out or recognize your accomplishments, just say "thank you." You know the dedication, sacrifice, and heartaches it takes to create your own luck. This will assist you in developing the burning desire to create your "luck" again for whatever you choose in the future. Continue to work hard and prepare for your future; you earn your luck.

These are examples of what can be done to create your own luck. These are examples of the "extra effort" things that can attract greatness to you.

Law of Human Behavior

Behavior is your conduct or action. Your behavior is how you act under certain circumstances. Human behavior can be an interesting topic. The way we behave demonstrates what we truly want, not what we say we want, out of life.

There are four primary components to human behavior:

1. **Thought**
2. **Physical Action**
3. **Feeling/emotion**
4. **Body Physiology**

All four of these affect each other and develop our behavior.

1. **Thoughts:** Your thoughts develop into your actions and feelings and influence your body function (your physiology). Positive thoughts initiate different actions, feelings, and physiology than negative thoughts. Positive thoughts create good feelings about yourself and others. Positive thoughts create positive actions and the physiology to build a strong, healthy body. Negative thoughts do the opposite.

2. **Physical Actions:** Your actions reinforce your thoughts, validate your feelings, and stimulate additional physiology, re-enforcing that thought.

3. **Feelings/emotions:** Your feelings or emotions are controlled by your reaction to your surroundings. Your feelings influence your actions, your thoughts, and your body's physiology.

4. **Body Physiology:** Your body releases different chemicals (hormones, etc.) in response to your thoughts, actions, and feelings. These influence your body's physiology and can influence your health. Positive experiences create health, and negative experiences inhibit health (create disease). Research has shown that prolonged negative thoughts lead to poor physiological effects such as anxiety, depression, and cancer. With positive thoughts we can help to eliminate these types of disease.

The Law of Human Behavior: Sooner or later we get exactly what we expect. Some people view this statement as a positive statement, while others view this as a negative statement. The people that see this as an optimistic or a positive statement, generally see the world more positively. Those that see this as a pessimistic or a negative statement, generally see the negatives of the world. Your thoughts are your choice. When looking at your future, you must ask yourself, "what do I want, and what do I expect out of myself to accomplish it?" What are you going to do, and how do you expect yourself to behave to meet your expectations? You must have expectations of yourself to achieve in any area of your life. Your expectations of yourself will mold your life. Some people's behavior destroys their own dreams. Some people's behavior support and assist in developing their dreams.

Example: Two people may have the dream of playing college baseball.

Person 1: Awakes four days per week at 5:20 a.m. and goes to the weight room at 6:00 a.m. to work on his strength, flexibility, endurance, coordination, agility, hitting, fielding, etc., until 7:30 a.m. This person also goes to baseball camps, stays after practice to work on individual skills, watches films of himself and others, meets with the coach to help him find colleges, etc.

Person 2: Awakes just in time to get to school, shows up to practice, and does not weight train or do any additional training besides what is required by the coach.

Which person is behaving like he wants to play college baseball? Which person will probably have a better chance of playing college baseball?

Person 1 is dedicated and making the sacrifices needed to play college baseball. He is "behaving" like a college baseball player.

Person 2 is just giving "lip service" to playing college baseball. This person may have the talent but not the dedication. He is not "behaving" like a college baseball player.

Every job that we perform is a self-portrait of us. If we give our best effort, we will never regret the outcome. Understand that without 100 percent commitment to doing what you want, there is no commitment at all.

If you like where you are at and what you are doing in life, then continue to do that and grow. If you want to change your life/destiny, you must change your thoughts, actions, feelings, and physiology. If you do this, it will change your behavior. This will change your destiny and your life.

We must think we can (Mental Law of Success), add physical action (Physical Law of Success), and then behave like we can (Law of Human Behavior) to achieve our dreams. This can be applied to every dream in our life.

Spiritual Law of Success

The Spiritual Law of Success: Everything you do comes back to you. If you put out good, you will receive good. If you put out bad, you will receive bad. You always get payback for what you do, one way or another, up to ten times in some books (such as the Bible). What I mean by this is if you steal $1.00 from a person it may cost you $10.00 in one form or another. I also believe the reverse is true. If you do something good (unconditionally, meaning you do it only because it is the right thing to do) for another person, I believe you can get paid back up to ten times with "goodness." This is an important concept to understand. Remember, do not "do" what you would "undo" if caught. Your consequence is the "playback" of the small voice within you that warned you not to do it in the first place. To receive greatness, you have to give greatness.

Law of Self-Talk

Self-talk is the daily mental conversation we have with ourselves. This is what we think about. How you talk to yourself is how you will think, act, and believe. Your "self-talk" can single-handedly shape your destiny. If I talked to you the way that you, many times, talk to yourself, you would hate me. Thoughts change lives. Are you your own "worst enemy" or your "biggest fan"? Self-talk changes lives. Make sure to think "why not?" instead of "can't." Think "abundance" instead of "lack." What are you going to be? Are you going to be an average person? An average person is the best of the worst and the worst of the best. Average is not like you. You are a high achiever. You have nothing to lose and everything to gain. Talk to yourself about your great opportunities and how great you are!

One thought can change a life. One positive thought thrown away or forgotten could be the thought that could have changed your life. A short pencil is better than a long memory. Write down your great thoughts and keep them in a file for the future.

How do you talk to yourself?
I am good.
I am fast.

I am strong.
I am quick.
I am smart.
People like me.
I like people.
I am polite, generous, and kind.
When I walk onto the field of competition I put on my "game face" and have the burning desire to do whatever I need to do within the rules of the game to win.
I am a winner.
I deserve to win.
I work hard.
Great things happen to me.
I deserve greatness.
I do great things for me and others.
Etc.

Self-talk will build or destroy your self-esteem. Positive self-talk will build your self-esteem. Until you have great self-esteem, you cannot truly "love" another person for who and what they are.

How do you control your self-talk?
You figure out solutions and do not dwell on problems.
You recognize the good in the world and not the bad.
You think of opportunities, not tragedies.

Your thoughts are your habits. Develop the habit of positive self-talk. Get excited about yourself! Get excited about your life! You've got great things ahead of you! You are a great person, and people like you. Your future starts with how you think of yourself. You have to get as excited about a "flat tire" as you do about opening a gift from a friend. This is difficult, I know. But it is a choice. Negative thoughts hold you back like an anchor around your waist. Get excited about you. You are awesome. You have wonderful traits, talents, and opportunities. You are smart, you are happy, and people like you. People want to be around you, and young people want to be like you. You must believe in yourself. Have a big dream, believe in yourself, have positive self-talk, add physical action, and you will achieve. You can change the world.

Master the Things that Do Not Take Talent

In life it is most important to "master the things that do not take talent." Once you do this, you can advance with the talents that you are given. These are called the fundamentals—the fundamentals of sport and/or the fundamentals of life. Example in athletics: Does it take any talent to hustle in a sport? Does it take any talent to box out in basketball? Does it take any talent to put your glove on the ground in baseball? Does it take any talent to have a good stance in football? These are the fundamentals. These are the things that must be mastered. Once you can master these things, then you can let your talents move you to the next level of achievement.

How does this work in life? Does it take any talent to be on time for your job? Does it take any talent to recognize the good in other people and tell them? Does it take any talent to see a pop can or piece of paper on the ground and pick it up and throw it away? Does it take any talent to say please and thank you? These things don't take talent. These things take discipline. Master these skills, and they will take you "light years" ahead in athletics and in life. Many times a person can overcome a lack of talent by mastering the things that do not require talent.

A less talented athlete can pass up an athlete with more talent if the more talented athlete does not master the things that do not require talent and the less talented athlete masters them. This is the same in life. A less talented person can have much more success than a more talented person if the less talented person masters basic life skills and the more talented person does not master these same basic life skills. These basic life skills consist of: respect for yourself and others; the ability to compliment, show gratitude, and show appreciation for others' strengths and weaknesses; being polite; recognizing the good in others, etc.

"Mastering the things that do not take talent" is one of the fundamentals of human interaction. Mastering these will assist you in achieving success. Mastering the things that do not require talent will catapult your life into the future.

Understanding Human Relationships

When you are growing up, up to ten years of age, you look at your parents like they know it all. They are the smartest; you may want to even marry your mom (if you are a young boy) or marry your dad (if you are a young girl).

As you mature, between the ages of eleven to fifteen, you start what I call the "why stage." This is where you start thinking or asking why your parents, friends, or relatives do certain things that do not make sense to you.

Why does he talk to me that way?
Why does she treat me that way?
Why does he always speed when he drives?
Why do I have to be home at midnight?
Why do I have to mow the yard?
Why do I have to stack the firewood?
Why do I have to shovel the walk?
Why does she always ask me about my grades?
Why does he always ask me about my practice?
WHY, WHY, WHY...

When you get to be sixteen to twenty-one years of age, you start what I call the "I can do better than them" or "they are stupid" stage of your development. This is a difficult stage between a parent and a teenager. The parent has had some life experiences that help them establish rules for the household, and the teenager wants to flex their "I am growing up" muscle. The teenager questions many things that the parents (or others in authority) tell them. The teenager feels they can do better than their parents, and they are going to prove it to them.

This is the "tipping point" to the long-term relationship of those individuals. The teenager and the parent must handle this correctly, or the long-term relationship may be tarnished for many years. The teenager must look inside to their integrity. If the teenager can see that the person in authority (parent, coach, or other) is trying to protect them, or position them to have fewer problems, then the teenager must trust that what they are telling them is correct and follow their judgment. If as a teenager, you choose not to follow their judgment and you "get caught," you have to accept the consequences of your actions. From the person in authority's side (parental/coach, etc.), you must let them make their own mistakes so they can learn from their experience. This is a difficult task for both sides. The teenager thinks he or she knows what is best, and the parents don't want the teenager to make the same mistakes that they made. We must go through this process to develop a great relationship.

Once you turn twenty-one to twenty-five years of age, you will look back at your life and think to yourself "they were not so stupid after all." If you make it through the above listed stages of development with respect for each other, you will have a wonderful long-term relationship with the people that you care about.

It is important to understand that you must go through these stages to develop a strong long-term relationship. You will go through this process in every meaningful human relationship that you will have: parent–child, boyfriend–girlfriend, coach–player, husband–wife, employer–employee, etc. In some instances, it will take years to go through this process (parent–child), and in others it may take just weeks (employer–employee). The important thing to understand is you must go through ALL of these stages to have a quality long-term relationship.

The people that have problems working through these stages end up going through multiple divorces, job jumping, and never reaching the level of success that they may dream of because they "pull the plug" and move in a different direction too fast. Understand you must go through this process. Understanding this process early in life will help you to understand where you are in your thought process when you feel frustration in the future. This is OK and normal to go through if you want something to work out for the long term. When you're feeling these emotions, ask yourself, "Where am I at in my development in this relationship? Do I want this relationship to last? Is this relationship worth maintaining? Is this person attempting to help me, or is he hindering me?" From this point, you will be able to understand where you are going and what lies ahead, and you will have less frustration with this relationship's development or termination.

The "red alert" in human relationships:
There is the rare occasion when an adult, significant other, or "person of authority" may "take advantage of this relationship" and attempt to lead a teenager or another person down the "wrong path." This usually begins with the person of authority "befriending" the teenager/person. After the person of authority has gained the trust of the other person, the person of authority belittles, degrades, points out the weaknesses of, and intimidates the other person, making him or her feel insignificant. Be careful of these people. These people can negatively affect your life, if you choose to allow them to. This is not a "healthy" situation. This type of relationship either needs to be addressed and changed or terminated. There is no "in-between." Remember, your path in life is established by your choices. Your morals, ethics, and values are established by you. If your morals, ethics, and values (whatever you choose them to be) are being violated by anyone, then you need to address the person that is violating your values and fix it, or terminate the relationship. Do not get trapped in an unhealthy relationship. It is unfortunate, but

some coaches, employers, parents, and people in general take this approach to relationship building, either knowingly or unknowingly. It is important that we recognize this, identify this as unacceptable behavior, and resolve it in one way or another. You are in control of your destiny. Do not be manipulated by others.

Understanding Futility

Futility is the identification of a useless situation or uselessness. Recognizing futility is one of life's hardest lessons—i.e., determining when something that we are doing is a waste of our time and/or energy, determining when "enough is enough." Examples of this could be a male/female relationship, a job/career, a hobby, a coach/athlete relationship, sport participation, or any other relationship/activity. This is a difficult situation, because there is no "right" answer. This really comes down to our individual level of "tolerance"; it is a "gut-feel."

To assist you in analyzing futility, I recommend the following. If your values, morals and ethics are being violated, then this is not a good situation for you to be in. You need to confront the situation to determine if the other person is willing or able to discontinue violating your values, morals, or ethics. If they are willing to make a change to not violate your values, morals, or ethics then it may be worth continuing that relationship. If they are not willing, or if they continue to violate your morals or ethics, you need to consider discontinuing that relationship.

There are many examples of demonstrating futility throughout life.

Examples:
Has your car broken down one too many times for you? Get a different car.
Has your roommate continued to eat your food without asking? Get a new roommate.
Has your girlfriend "cut you down" one too many times? Get a new girlfriend.
Has your boss been rude to you for the last time? Get a new job.
And the list goes on.

Everyone's tolerance is different. One person may perceive an automobile as a "piece of junk," and another person may see this same automobile as a "diamond in the rough." The difference usually is in a level of understanding of the situation. A person who does not know much about how to fix an automobile may have less tolerance for that automobile than a person who understands how to fix it. Therefore, there is a different perception of the automobile from one person to another.

Those people that have very little tolerance for outside circumstances, people, and situations tend to "jump around" from job to job, partner to partner, friend to friend, college to college, etc. I encourage you to have patience with yourself and others. Do not give up too early, and do not allow yourself to be used or abused. This is all a judgment call by you. Again, recognizing futility is one of life's toughest lessons; there is no right or wrong answer.

Failing Forward

It has been stated you "fail your way to success." Remember, in life there is no failure, just feedback. How you respond to that feedback will determine your level of success. There is always a time to say enough is enough and change your momentum in a different direction. This is called "futility." You can change a school, change your career or job, etc. That will be your call. This is an internal decision and is nothing more then a "feel." Understand what failure is not:

1. **Avoidable**—We all will fail sometime in our lives. Many of us will fail a lot more in some areas than others.
2. **An event**—You don't just have something happen to you one day, and now you are a failure!
3. **Objective**—Yes, you can fail a test, but that doesn't make you a failure!
4. **The enemy**—Failure is not a bad thing. It helps us to see what does not work so we can make a change and see what will work.
5. **Irreversible**—Once you make a mistake, you can always change what you did and anticipate a different result. To do the

same thing and expect a different result could be considered a form of insanity.

6. **A stigma**—Failure does not "just follow you around," but you can attract it depending on how you think. There are common sayings that people have to attract negativity to them. Examples: Failure comes in 3s. You have a black cloud following you around. What you say/think is what you get.

7. **Final**—When you fail it does not make you a failure, or a failure for the rest of your life.

Failures are not final. You will always gain one thing by striving for a goal. That one thing is experience. You may not always reach your dream or goal, but you will always gain experience by having a dream or goal. Obstacles are placed in front of us to determine how much we want something. If you truly want something, "do not point a finger" at anyone else but yourself. If you reach an obstacle, do not complain. If you truly want it, work harder!

In order to succeed, we must fail; just make sure you "fail forward." Failure is the price we pay to achieve success. Learn from your successful failures.

Be Honest

Honesty is the ability to not deceive, steal, or take advantage of the trust of others. It is important to be honest with others, but is also important to be honest with yourself. For example, if you're not happy with your playing time, have you done all you can to be "playable"? Have you made it to all the practices? Did you practice in the off-season? Are you doing the "extras" that the others are? When something is not going your way, take a quick look "within" to see if there is something you can do to make a change. Too many times people look to blame others. Many times in our lives we will have the opportunity to test our honesty with our friends, parents, family, and ourselves. Make the right choice when being tested. Anyone who thinks they can go to the top and stay there without being honest is only fooling themselves. He or she who loses his or her honesty has nothing else to lose.

Have Self-Confidence

Self-confidence is the ability to rely on yourself, confident that you have the capacity to make the right choices and/or get the job done. "If it's going to be, it's up to me." The starting point for both success and happiness is a healthy self-image. This simply means to be confident about your abilities and your ability to make the right choices. Walk with a swagger. You have learned a great deal. You have had a great number of experiences, thanks to the people that care about you (friends, family, coaches, etc.). With that being said, you also have a lot to learn, master, and improve upon. Believe in yourself. Do not be "cocky." There is a fine line between being self-confident and "cocky." To be confident is to "walk the walk and fill the talk." When your self-image improves, your performance improves. To be a good/great person you must be confident in your abilities. One of the key factors that distinguishes self-confidence from "cockiness" is the ability to compliment others. The person that can give and receive compliments in a sincere, genuine manner will have less chance of being perceived as arrogant (cocky). When your confidence improves, your competence improves at the same time. To improve your self-image and self-confidence, do something nice for someone else.

Have Self-Control

Self-control is the ability to control your emotions and your actions, think through your options, choose the best option, and do not act impulsively. Many times the problem is not what happens to you, but how you react to what happens you. Self-control is a difficult thing at times but is vital to long-term success. Self-control is a choice.

Have Self-Responsibility

Self-responsibility is the act of being responsible for yourself. Self-responsibility is having control over your actions and taking responsibility for the outcome, good or bad. Self-responsibility is standing on your own "two feet" and not blaming others for your successes or failures. Self-responsibility is making our own choices and not blindly following others. Self-responsibility is being dependant on yourself to succeed.

Be Enthusiastic

Enthusiasm is a passionate expression of interest. The ability to be enthusiastic is the ability to celebrate loudly and with great emotion. This builds momentum for great things in life. In athletic events, great changes in momentum occur and can "make or break" a team. The team that can keep and maintain enthusiasm is the team that will control the momentum of the game and will have the advantage in the end. Thus is the same with life. Celebrate loudly, with a lot of positive body language, and you will have the advantage in life. Enthusiasm is contagious; unfortunately so is the lack of it. To be enthusiastic, you have to act enthusiastically. Enthusiasm is a key to a successful, happy life.

Self-Discipline

Self-discipline is the ability to accomplish what is necessary in order to reach your goal. It means executing what you know needs to be done even when you "don't feel like doing it." Other words for self-discipline are: determination, work ethic, dedication, etc. It means having the self-discipline to reach what you have set out to accomplish even if it becomes difficult. When the going gets tough, the tough get going. Work ethic has been explained with a glass and grains of sand. The glass is your individual "Life Potential." All glasses (Life Potentials) are different sizes and shapes. This demonstrates that everybody's potential is different. Using athletics for an example, the grain of sand is used to acknowledge every time you do something to enhance your athletic potential (make yourself better), for examples: lift weights, increase your flexibility, train in a skill, etc. Each time you work to make yourself better it is like adding one small grain of sand to the glass. The goal is to have your glass (athletic potential) as full as possible to reach your maximum athletic potential at a specific time. What this means is the harder you work when you're young, the "more full your glass" and the better you will be when you're older. Thus, how good you are now has no relationship with how good you could be when you are senior in high school, in college, or if you're lucky enough, professionally. Understand that being self-disciplined, dedicating yourself to athletics, and having a strong work ethic will get the maximum out of your athletic potential. This same analogy can be used in all areas of life: marriage, a job/career, building a family, being a father or a mother, etc. Remember that other people, things, and situations can stop you temporarily, but you are the only one that can stop yourself permanently. Self-discipline, determination, and persistence are three keys to working through the hurdles of life and achieving success.

Confronting

To confront is to address or deal with a situation, problem, or issue. Confronting another individual can be a difficult task. Mastering the ability to confront others in a productive manner will bring you farther down the road of success. You'll have many opportunities to confront others throughout your life. Confrontation is not easy, but it is sometimes necessary to get your questions answered. Here are some guides to follow when confronting others:

1. It is not easy to confront others, and it is okay to be nervous.
2. If you are emotional (angry, upset, etc.), do not confront the situation until you have your emotions under control.
3. Ask to speak with the person one-on-one in a private location.
4. When asking the questions, be calm, confident, and non-emotional and look them directly in the eyes.
5. When the person is answering you, look him/her directly in the eyes and let them know when you understand. You may not like or agree with the answer, but at least now you understand. Now you have the opportunity to accept or debate

the response until you and the other person have worked out the situation to a resolution.

You may or may not like the answer you receive. However, chances are the person will respect you for confronting the situation, and you will feel better about yourself for confronting the situation and putting it to rest. Confronting is the ability to get the answers to your questions. It is not easy, but many times it is necessary.

Responding to Negativity

Negativity exists throughout the world. Understanding how to deal with negativity is a key to life. Negativity can be a death spiral for life. There are two outcomes that can occur in response to negativity. One is the negative comment or situation, and the second is a negative response to that comment or situation. Understand that the best response to any negative comment is "no response." When you don't respond, the negative comment has nowhere to go. Providing "no response" is like "throwing water on the fire." Giving a response to the negative comment is like "throwing gas on a fire." The best response to a negative response is "no response." Look the person in the eye, keep your mouth shut, walk away, and do your job. Remember, it is not what happens to you that is the problem, but how you react to what happens to you that can be the problem. If you could "kick" the person responsible for most of your troubles, you would probably not be able to "sit down" for a week. The best response to negativity is no response!

Choice

Choice is to select or choose. We all make choices on a daily basis; some are easy, and some are more difficult. The choices we make dictate the life we live. The choices we make establish our reputation and our character. Our character is the most important thing we will ever own. Our reputation is how people perceive us. Our character is how we perceive ourselves. When making the "hard choices," consider your consequences. Weigh out the good and the bad, the positives and negatives; then make your choice. The choices we make affect others. Some choices affect more people than other choices. Make sure when making your choices that you consider all those who could possibly be affected. Make the "right choice" even when it is the "hard choice." It is not always easy, but the "right choice" is a direct result of your character.

Be "At Choice"

To be "At Choice" means that you are in charge of your choices. This means you are making the decisions for your life. You are not blindly following anyone down the road of life. It means that you will be making your decisions and taking responsibility for your actions, be it good or bad. To be "At choice" means: "If it is going to be, it is up to me" (NOT someone else). This means you are in charge of your life and your destiny. It is difficult to always make the right choice. We all make mistakes. When making the "hard choices," always look to your values. If you look to your values, more often then not you will make the "right choice" even when it is the "hard choice." In life it is most important to be "At Choice."

Character vs. Reputation

Your character is your individual qualities/traits that build your personal individuality. Your character is how you react to different situations. Your reputation is how others see you. Your character and your reputation are based on the choices you make. Your reputation is how people interpret you and your behavior. Your character is how you see yourself. Are you honest, giving, helpful, truthful, humble? Are you a bully, dishonest, arrogant, a taker, not helpful? These are all character traits. Your character is built on what you stand for. Your reputation is built on what you fall for. Difficult times build and expose your character. Your ability can take you to the top, but it is your character that will keep you there.

Perseverance

Perseverance is the ability to continue your efforts in spite of opposition or resistance. Perseverance allows you to fulfill your dream and not allow other people/things to get in your way. Success is achieved by those who "try and keep trying." Perseverance is all the hard work that you do, after all of the hard work you have done. Many people that have kept trying, even when it felt hopeless, ended up developing some of life's most precious treasures. In order to achieve great dreams you will need perseverance. Understanding perseverance will help you get through the tough times and cherish your successes!

Communicate Well to Lead

Communication is giving or passing information. It is the ability to have others understand one's ideas. There are many forms of communication: verbal, body language, facial expressions, and the list goes on. Understanding the "communication loop" is important. The "communication loop" consists of giving information, receiving/comprehending the information, and then applying it. If the "communication loop" is not made, then there are "loose ends." If there are "loose ends," then miscommunication occurs, and frustration builds from the giver of the information and to the receiver of the information. To form the communication loop, three things must occur:

1. There must be information given.
2. There must be acknowledgment that the information was received and understood.
3. There must be action taken. You must do what you are asked to do. This is the application of the information.

If the acknowledgment that the information was received and understood is not communicated back to the giver of the information, or if the receiver of the information does not do what the giver asked, it is normal human behavior for the giver of the information to become louder, more direct, and less compassionate. The "communication loop" was not fulfilled, which leads to frustration. The conversation then turns into yelling.

Communication is a two-way street: the giving of information and the receiving of information. *How* the information is given and *how* the information is received is as important as the information itself. Understand, there are three components of the "communication loop":

1. The giving of information
2. The receiving of information
3. The application of that information.

Communication is a key component to many areas of life.

The Art of Meeting Another Person

Meeting another person is a form of communication. It is often said there is only one chance to make a first impression. The way you meet others has a great chance of influencing their opinion of you. It is important that you learn how to meet other people in a confident and respectful manner.

Remember to:

1. Look the person directly in their eyes.
2. Smile.
3. Introduce yourself using your first and last name.
4. Shake their hand with a firm handshake.
5. Recognize something good about them and tell them. (Compliment them)
6. Ask questions about them. People know most about themselves.
7. At the end of the conversation, "bow out" gracefully by looking them directly in the eyes and saying something like this: "It was great meeting you, John." Use their name, shake their hand with the firm handshake, smile, and say, "Have a nice day."

The Power of the Compliment

A compliment is a verbal expression of courteous praise demonstrating respect. To compliment, is to recognize the good in others and, most importantly, tell them. It is best to compliment people in front of others. Be loud with compliments and quiet with criticisms. Compliments build self-esteem for the person giving and the person receiving the compliment. Compliments feel good to give and receive. Everyone likes to receive compliments, but few people give them. I am not sure why this is. It feels great giving someone a compliment. Some people think that by giving someone a compliment, it could bring out arrogance in the person receiving the compliment. By giving a compliment, it actually creates positive feelings for both the giver and the receiver. If you want to receive compliments, then give them freely and genuinely. When giving a compliment, look the person directly in the eyes and compliment them in a warm, sincere voice. To receive a compliment, simply say, "thank you." Please do not come up with excuses or ignore the compliment. Recognizing the good in others and telling them is great for you and them. A sincere compliment is one of the most effective motivational tools in existence. The surest way to knock a chip off of someone's shoulder is to give them a pat on the back. Compliments help both the giver and the receiver to achieve.

Dealing with Jealousy/Envy

Envy is a painful or resentful awareness of an advantage enjoyed by another person, followed by the desire to possess the same advantage. This destructive feeling leads to jealousy.

Dealing with jealousy can be very difficult for everyone involved. Take the example of a more talented and a less talented athlete. There are many pressures that come with success. For the athlete that is very talented or gifted in a particular sport, "jealousy" may develop among other athletes or other athletes' parents. The more talented athlete's parents may appear to be very proud of their athlete and make comments indicating that their athlete may be more superior than others on the team. This can be a sensitive situation for the parents whose athlete may not be in the "spotlight." The less talented athlete (or the athlete's parents) may become "jealous" of the other athlete's success. This may start a "jealousy pattern" of belittling, pointing out weakness, and degrading the more talented athlete. This can destroy a team from within. One of the best ways to combat this is to have the more talented athlete and his or her parents recognize the good in the other athletes around them, and tell them! This comes down to the "compliment." By receiving compliments from the more talented player, the less talented player (and parents) will be inclined to show less jealousy. This will lead to more team support and less team division.

This concept can be applied to many areas of life. People can become jealous of each other for multiple reasons. Please remember, if you want to get along with other people, recognize the good in them.

Be Coachable/Teachable

Being coachable/teachable is having the ability to be coached/taught. It is the ability to listen to your coach/teacher and apply what is being taught. Ask questions if needed, but don't talk back or be disrespectful to your coach/teacher. This type of behavior will only hurt the coach/athlete, teacher/student relationship. This is a lose–lose situation. Do things the way the coach/teacher is teaching you and not your way. To be coachable/teachable is to have the desire to willingly make the changes that will improve your life. Being coachable/teachable is having the ability to listen, learn, and apply what you have been taught.

You Determine Your Level of Success

Success is the achievement of something intended or desired. There are many definitions of success. Your level of personal success should only be determined by you. Success is achieved by reaching your optimal potential. Your success will be determined by achieving your personal goals and dreams. You are the only one that can determine if you are successful. Success is achieved by those who try and keep trying. You already have every characteristic you need to succeed. Establish your dreams and goals, make a plan, add physical action, and succeed. All people want to succeed. Some people want to succeed so bad that they are even willing to work for it. None of the "secrets of success" will work unless you do. I am confident that one day you can be successful. It is all up to you. Remember one thing, it is sometimes harder to *be* a success than it is to *become* a success. Successful people maintain their success with their honesty, integrity, and respect for themselves and others. Successful people maintain their success by maintaining their character.

Lead Others

Leadership is the ability to show the way, to guide or direct others. Many people feel that leadership at a young age is "just developed." In my opinion, leadership is a learned behavior. Some of the important people in my life have stated that leadership is actually helpfulness. Helpfulness is the ability to help and serve others. I think great leadership has multiple traits. Some of them are helpfulness, gratitude, honesty, integrity, truthfulness, respect, perseverance, self-control, and the ability to "move on" when hurdles are in your way. This ability to "move on" has been termed "indomitable spirit."

Great leadership is built on quality morals and ethics. Many people want to be led; the question is where are they being led? Are they being led down a road of success, or are they being led down a road of adversity and suffering?

In order to lead people down the road of success, a leader needs to possess a set of distinctive traits that I like to call the six C's:

1. **Courage**—this is the courage to move forward in spite of circumstances.

2. **Competence**—people need to believe this person is smart enough or qualified enough to lead them.
3. **Candor**—this is being sincere, speaking to people from the heart, and being truthful.
4. **Commitment**—to have trust that their leader is going to follow through to the end.
5. **Compassion**—to have feelings for others in good times and bad; to help celebrate the good and offer counsel for the bad.
6. **Communication**—this is the ability to exchange information, to give information, have others understand the information, and be willing to apply what is communicated.

Strong leaders use the six C's to accomplish what needs to be accomplished. Leaders lead, and from these six C's followers develop confidence and trust in their leadership to create many of life's miracles.

In order to follow a leader, people need to understand that their leader has these six distinctive traits. Understanding these traits will assist you in developing your leadership skills.

Control Your Attitude to Achieve

Attitude is a state of thought or feeling. Your attitude is your mental state. Your attitude is moldable. Your attitude is your choice. Your attitude can only be changed by you, but can be influenced by much/many. Your attitude is your outlook on the world at that point in time. Your attitude is either optimistic (positive) or pessimistic (negative). There is no in-between. Your attitude will project what you want. Here's an example. In order to find a good friend, you'll have to be a good friend. Changing your attitude will dramatically change your performance. If you think you can, you will! Ask yourself, "Is my attitude worth catching?" Remember, it is your attitude, not your aptitude (intelligence), that will determine your altitude (level of success). Your attitude is more important than your aptitude. When people ask you how you are, you can respond with, "I'm fantastic, but I'll get better." Of all the things you "wear," your attitude is the most important.

Our attitude is the single, most important thing that can determine our level of success and our outcome in life.

Attitude of Gratitude

Gratitude is a thankful appreciation for something received. Gratitude is simply appreciating the "people" and "things" around you and showing it. This may be as simple as saying "thank you." It is easy to take people/things for granted. It is easy to get caught up in yourself. But remember, nobody ever "makes it on their own." There are people who give you the opportunity to achieve. There are literally hundreds of people who wait on you daily. They may get paid for it, or they may not. They all deserve to be appreciated. This takes very little time, effort, or thought, and is very much appreciated by the people around you.

Here's how it works:

"Mom, thank you for bringing me to practice today."
"Teacher X, thank you for teaching us about math today; I enjoyed that".
"Coach, thanks for helping us with our offense today; I think I got it."
"Janitor X, thank you for cleaning up after us each day; without you we would have a pretty messy school."

"Principal X, thank you for keeping our school organized and on track. I appreciate you."

"Dad, thank you for going to work everyday and providing us with the things that we need to live the way we live."

Spouse to spouse, "Thank you for making dinner tonight."

Employer to employee, "Thank you for coming into work today; it is going to be a great day."

This is simple stuff, BUT it is easy to have expectations of the people we are closest to and to overlook the need to appreciate them. This can make that person feel "taken advantage of." A common quote for this is "stop and smell the roses." I like to say "stop and smell the roses, and thank the person who planted them."

Remember, nobody has to do anything for anybody. If people know that you sincerely appreciate them, they will do more for you than you can possibly imagine. Think about the people around you and recognize them for the good they do. It does not take long or a tremendous amount of energy. It is amazing how good it will make you feel to recognize others for the great things that they do for all of us.

Two ways to develop gratitude:

1. Establish a "Gratitude Journal" and write in it on a daily basis. Before bed is best. Write three to five great things that happened to you that day and see the difference in your life. Great things will continue to happen to you!

2. Write "Letters of Gratitude." Write a letter telling someone that you appreciate all the great things that they do or have done for you. It is best to hand-deliver it and then read it to the person that you wrote it to. If you cannot do that, then mail or email it to them for them to enjoy on their own. It is healthy to feel important in the lives of others. Showing your appreciation is a great way to spread "good" in the world.

Acknowledging the "good" in the world will create more "good" in the world—this is the Spiritual Law of Success.

Walking Between the Lines

Walking between the lines is an attitude. Simply stated, it is the expected changes that occur in your attitude and behavior in different environments. To help you understand this better, you may need to be aware that certain changes are expected of you when you are in different situations in your life. Everybody acts differently in different environments. Understanding how you are supposed to act in those environments is critical for you to reach your maximum potential. For example, as parents we all want our kids to be nice, polite people off of the floor, mat, field, etc. When an athlete steps on the floor, mat, field, etc., we, as parents and coaches, expect them to turn on a switch of desire, passion, mental toughness, self-discipline, coachability, self-confidence, and focus that will bring their game to the next level. Understand that this is no different than turning on a switch when you walk into any other environment. For example, when you walk into church, think about how you're supposed to act. Now take that same switch and put it on the basketball floor, football field, hockey arena, or wrestling mat. Think about how you are supposed to act. Let's use an extreme example: on the football field you are asked to be loud and tackle or block others. In church you are to keep quiet, listen, and not touch others. Let's say you tackled the priest as he was giving his sermon. How would tackling the priest be interpreted by others? Not good, I know. I understand that this is an extreme example, but the concept is the same. People who master the ability to understand what is expected of them in different environments can have unlimited potential. This situation can be applied to band, choir, employment, recreation, classroom, and many other activities. As we get older, this is applied in all areas of our lives. In athletics it is known as "putting on your game face." In everyday life it is commonly known as "changing your hat." Winning is not the only thing, but putting forth your best effort to win is. Many times the difference in your success or failure is in your attitude. The concept behind "Walking Between the Lines" helps you to determine the type of attitude you need to portray in different environments.

Sell Yourself

It is important to "sell yourself." Some people confuse selling themselves with bragging. Bragging is talking about yourself with disregard for other people. When people ask questions about you, give them enough information/detail to "spark" their curiosity. Wait a few seconds to see if they have any more questions and then ask questions about them. People will not know who you are, what you do, what you like, or what your talents are, if you do not tell them. When people ask you a question like how is school going, how is a sport going, etc. they would like an answer in detail. To answer "good" does not answer their question. They want to know about you. They want to understand what your likes and dislikes are. They want to know if they have anything in common with you. If it is a coach, teacher, or employer, they are trying to position you the best way they can to benefit their system. In order to get the best out of you or get the best out of their system, they need to understand what your strengths and weaknesses are. You will get your time to "prove yourself," but in the beginning you must "sell yourself" to get the opportunity to "prove yourself." A coach, teacher, or employer must have some curiosity about what you can do to give you the opportunity to "prove it." You can "spark" their curiosity by telling them about your accomplishments. This "spark" can give you the opportunity to "prove yourself." This can open many doors in your future.

Life Balance

As we get older, time demands change. We go from focusing primarily on your own personal needs (college, athletics, relationships, etc.) to focusing on our personal needs AND the needs of our job/career, then possibly a spouse, and then a family. Many people struggle with balancing their lives. If you feel stressed, then it is a hint that your life is out of balance. To help you with decreasing the stress and getting back closer to balance, here is a concept that may help. There are five primary and two secondary areas that people must keep in balance to feel they have control of their lives.

Primary:

1. **Spiritual**
2. **Physical**
3. **Intellectual**
4. **Emotional**
5. **Cultural**

Spiritual: This is your relationship with a higher power. Are you worshiping your higher power on a regular basis so your higher power can assist you in accomplishing your goals? Are you becoming educated by your higher power on how to be a great human being? This is a sense of spiritual well-being that can easily be put by the wayside. It is sometimes easy to forget to get the information from the place that truly has control of your destiny.

Physical: This is keeping your health and staying in good shape. When you're young it is fairly easy to keep in good shape, especially for young athletes. This keeps you in good physical condition because of your motivation to perform at your highest level. Because of this, you are more focused on eating well, exercising with strength training, aerobic activity, agility training, explosive power training, flexibility training, etc. As you get older and time demands change, this may get more difficult. Remember to keep your body in good physical condition.

Intellectual: This is basically doing what you have to do to gather as much intelligence as you need, to do what you want to do, etc. It is easy when in college to maintain your intelligence, because you are in a "learning mode." As you get into your job or career, make sure to continue your learning. A mind that is learning is an "open mind."

Emotional: This can be difficult for some. This is keeping your emotions "in check." This has to do with the tone of your voice and your reaction to other people. If you see yourself getting angry often, crying, or looking at the negative of the world, you need to change your response. Emotions are 100 percent under our control. Emotions are our reactions to an outside stimulus that many times we have no control over. We can choose to be mad because it rained and we wanted to do something outside, but that does not help the situation. We cannot do anything about the weather. Emotions are under our control. If you feel yourself having poor emotional behavior, then it is up to you to change that. It is a choice.

Cultural: This is the ability to expose yourself to something different than what you may normally do. This is going to a play, to a choir concert, pig hunting, fishing, to a softball game, etc. This is doing something that you normally do not do on a daily, weekly, monthly, or even an annual basis.

Secondary:

1. **Motivational**
2. **Financial**

Motivational: This is what stimulates you to get out of bed in the morning and do something productive with your life. This may be motivational audio books, college, athletics, career, etc. You may feel yourself "bored" with what you are doing or feel lazy. That is OK for short periods of time, BUT if you feel that and you look back and thirty days have passed, then pick up a motivational book, CD/DVD, or tape and start changing your life. Remember, if it is going to be, it is up to me. Do not blame others; take control of your life.

Financial: This can be a big stressor for many people. It becomes a stressor for one primary reason. Some people live paycheck to pay check and do not plan for their future. The sooner you save money for your future, the faster you will be able to retire with all of the things that you want to have and enjoy so you can live your life to the fullest. If you do what you need to do when you need to do it, someday you will be able to do what you want to do when you want to do it.

If you feel yourself "stressed," it is important to look back at these seven areas and figure out which one(s) you're focused on "a lot" and which ones you are focused on very little. Start doing more in the areas that you are "letting slide." You will begin to feel much better about yourself and your accomplishments. You will feel much less "stressed," and you will accomplish more.

Life balance is a key in dealing with the stresses of life!

Dream BIG Dreams

Dreams are free. If you are going to dream, DREAM HUGE DREAMS! Make them bigger than you could almost imagine. Have dreams in many areas of your life. What kind of career do you dream of? What type of family do you dream of having? What do you want to do with your family? What do you want to accomplish in your life? Etc. It is better to shoot for the stars and land on the moon than to shoot for the moon and land on the barn.

There is a difference between a dream and a wish. A dream is a burning desire buried deep in your soul. A wish is just a "short-lived" emotion that sounds good but for which you are not willing to work or sacrifice to achieve. A dream is something that is hard for you to stop thinking about, something you are willing to give up your time, energy, and money to accomplish. A dream is something for which you will do whatever it takes to make it happen. Temporary setbacks are looked on as small hurdles. You can work through the hurdles and learn from your mistakes. This can make accomplishing your dream even more fulfilling. If you do not have a dream, how can you have a dream come true? Dreams will help you build an exceptional life. Have great dreams!

Have a Plan for Your Life

A plan for your life is like a road map. Many people have a more detailed plan when they go to the grocery store or on a trip than they do for the most important thing that they have: their life. Start out with a dream or many dreams. Establish a plan on how to accomplish these dreams. Write it down, or you will forget. A short pencil is better then a long memory. Write down the things you will have to do to accomplish your dream. Write it down in as much detail as you can imagine. Set goals on what you have to do to reach your dream. These goals will eventually get you to your dream. The goals are the map to direct you to accomplish your dream. If you were in Wisconsin and wanted to drive to Florida, would you just get in your car and start driving, OR would you look at a map? Most would look at a map and plan their route. This is the same as planning your life. Make a map. Many people plan vacations, plan their grocery list, plan their week, BUT they forget to plan the most important thing they have: their life. Make a plan for your life. If you fail to plan, it is a plan to fail.

Have Goals—Will Travel

Goals help you accomplish your dreams. If you have goals, you will travel. Goals are "benchmarks" that lead you to accomplishing your dream. Goals are the steps you have to accomplish to get to your dreams. If you were traveling from Wisconsin to Florida, the goals are like the towns that are traveled through to get to Florida. When traveling, do we just read the map once and not look at it again? Most do not. They study the map to find the best way to go, taking into consideration many things such as the fastest way, the size of the towns they will be traveling through, the type of road they will be traveling on, the speed limit on that road, etc. We need to treat our personal goals the same way to accomplish our dreams. We need to study our goals. Find the best (not necessarily the fastest) way to accomplish our dream. We need to review our goals often to make sure we are on track and traveling in the right direction. If we run into detours when accomplishing our dreams, we need to be able to adjust the plan to reach our dreams. The plan is the path to get to each goal. Have goals. Have LOTS of goals. Have a plan to reach each goal. Use the five primary and two secondary areas of "life balance," have dreams, set goals, and achieve a great life.

Understanding Your Career or Job

Your career or job is a vehicle to your personal goals. The people that turn their career or their job into a "way of life" can end up with poor personal and family relationships. Choosing a job/career is very important and should be carefully thought through. Some people get very "wrapped up" in their job/career and forget about the two important things they have: their health and their family. It is easy to choose career over the things you need to do to be healthy and have a happy family. Sometimes you have to. But if you consistently choose career over health and family, you will be quite disappointed in the end. If you lose your health or your family, nobody is happy. Remember, your job or career is the vehicle to your personal goals and dreams. Have dreams, set your goals, and use your career or job to assist you in your quest to achieve your dreams. Always remember to "maintain" your health and your family.

Be a Public Speaker

Public speaking can be intimidating. Public speaking is a great way to communicate to groups of people. Many people do not or will not speak in front of large groups. Public speaking is one way to help people learn. You can also position yourself as an "authority" in the area you are speaking about. Public speaking will help you motivate yourself, your teammates, and other community members. Public speaking can change people's lives. Public speaking can encourage others to help themselves or to help you. Public speaking is a great way to motivate others to make a change in their lives.

Be Humble

Humility is the state of being humble. Being humble is the ability to not get caught up in ones accomplishments, to not have "a big head," to not be arrogant. Humility has some specific traits such as being able to apologize, being able to listen, being grateful, being able to forgive, not holding a grudge, etc. This is called being "transparent." This means people can see who you are. This means their first impression is usually the right impression. Humility is the ability to share and enjoy the good things that happen to you with the people who helped make it happen.

Have Respect for Yourself and Others

Respect is a special consideration that you hold for a person or thing. If you want the respect of others, show respect to them. The term respect is very broad and can be used in almost all aspects of life. The following are some examples of respect: being polite and using words such as please and thank you; looking a person squarely in the eyes when they are talking to you; looking interested when a person is speaking to you; taking your shoes off at the door when visiting another person's house; calling people Mr. or Mrs.; not littering. These are all forms of respect. Respect is a habit that will take you far into the future if you chose to use it. Disrespect will hold you back like an anchor holding back a boat in the water! It is important to have respect for other people and other things. It is most important to have respect for yourself.

Have High Integrity

Integrity is the ability to maintain "moral soundness." Moral soundness means the ability to determine right from wrong and make the correct choice. Integrity is doing the "right thing" even when no one is watching. Integrity is doing the "right thing" even when it is difficult. If you have to "stand alone" to maintain your moral soundness, "stand alone." Integrity is your ability to make the right choices for the right reasons. Some phrases that are used to describe integrity are truthfulness, truth seeking, striving for excellence, diligence, etc. Ralph Waldo Emerson stated it best when he said, "what lies behind us and what lies before us are tiny matters compared to what lies within us." A high level of integrity will give you health, happiness, security, a restful night sleep and will propel you into the future.

Understanding Team

A team is an interesting concept. A team is bringing together people with different backgrounds, morals, ethics, life experiences, etc., for the purpose of achieving a common goal. Because of all of the variables involved in a team, half of the battle is getting that team to work together. Too often teams play as a group of individuals. When a team plays as a group of individuals, they usually are more focused on their own performance rather than the performance of the team. This is the group of individuals who would rather hit three home runs and lose than to "go hitless" and win. It is important to track statistics for both individuals and teams, but never put individual statistics ahead of team statistics. In most teams there is a group of more talented athletes and a group of less talented athletes. It is important to remember that every person will have an opportunity to succeed based on what they contribute to the team. A teammate's only job may be to participate in practice. This is that individual's contribution to the team's success. Some teammates may be in the "spotlight" more than others. Understand, this is part of the game; you cannot have a team without all of the players. A team has reached "true success" when all players can celebrate and feel great about their individual successes *and* the sacrifices each player has contributed to create the success of the team. Every dog has his day. The true success of the team is when everyone feels great about the individual accomplishments that were created and when they've achieved the team goal.

To have a good team, you have to be a good teammate. A good teammate demonstrates the characteristics of honesty, integrity, and respect. If a teammate has these three characteristics he/she will be able to demonstrate the three team characteristics of truthfulness, humility, and unselfishness that are critical for team success. Many people think of teams mostly in regards to athletics. Understand that you will take part in many teams in your future, not just in athletics. A team may consist of a job, career, relationship with your wife/ girlfriend, or the development of a family. Understanding the concept of a team and how to be a great teammate can create much success in your future. Remember that coming together is the beginning, staying together is work in progress, and working together for a common goal is success.

Dealing with Mistakes

A mistake is an error, blunder, or doing something wrong. At some point in time you will be wrong. It is OK to make mistakes. It is NOT OK to not take responsibility for your actions and to not forgive yourself. Remember to love yourself and others unconditionally. Unconditionally means to love people for "who they are," not for what they have, what they have accomplished, or what their name is.

We all make mistakes. When you make a mistake, do the following seven steps in no specific order:

1. Tell the truth.
2. Sincerely apologize. Say, "I am sorry. I made a mistake, and it will not happen again."
3. Accept responsibility. "It was my fault. I take responsibility for my actions."
4. Make it right if possible. Fix the situation the best you can (pay for damages, repair it, etc).
5. If you have one, ask for your higher power's forgiveness (God, etc.).
6. Forgive yourself.
7. Move on and do not dwell on your mistakes.

This process is "easier said then done." I do promise that if you follow this process, recovering from your mistakes will go much smoother than if you do not follow these steps.

When a person has "wronged you," remember to forgive them and move on. Do not "hate." To "hate" will bring on more of what you "hate" (The Spiritual and Mental Laws of Success).

Understanding the Basics of Money

Poor money management and financial stress can be a stressor that can consume you and destroy relationships. There are many temptations with money. If you have money, people want you to spend it, so they can have it. If you do not have money, people want you to borrow it so they can make money from your money. To follow are some basic concepts to help you with your money management.

If you ever have to choose between making money by compromising your morals, ethics, or core values and losing money while maintaining your morals, ethics, and core values—lose the money.

"Live on" less money than you make. If you can do this then you can invest your money to make more money. This is called "having your money work for you." If you "spend more than you make" then you will be a slave to the things that you have. Live on less now, and have your money work for you so you can live on more later and work less for the things you need or want.

Rule of 72.
This is a rule that helps you see how "interest" can work for you and against you.

If you have $100.00 and get 8% APR interest on it, how long will it take for that $100.00 to double to $200.00?
You take the number 72 and divide it by the interest rate. This number will give you how long it takes for the dollar amount to double.

Example:
This is how this can work for you in money accumulation.
72/interest rate (APR)

72 / 8 = 9 years for the dollar amount to double.

This can also work against you with a loan: If you have a $100.00 loan at 8% interest, how long will it take the loan to double?

72 / 8 = 9 years for the loaned amount ($100.00) to double ($200.00).

The Rule of 72 is a general rule that can assist you when thinking about debt reduction and money accumulation.

Credit cards:
Get a credit card that does not charge a monthly fee and only charges interest on the balance that is carried forward each month. Pay off your credit card each month in full. Credit cards are high-interest items that can rob you of your wealth.

Types of income:
Career income—The money you make from performing your career.

Passive income—The money you make by investing your career income into income-producing ventures (monthly rental properties, stock market investing, etc.)

Trade or Business—A "trade or business" is a business that you are actually involved in. The key to this type of arrangement is you must work at least five hundred hours per year in the trade or business, and nobody must work more than you and your family in this business.

(Examples: weekly rental properties, a coffee shop, a restaurant, or any income-producing business). Another key to this is you must attempt to "make" money doing the "job" and not just "lose" money to get money back on taxes.

There are limitations to "passive income" from a tax basis. In a "trade or business" there is more freedom to write things off, and it can put you in a better tax situation. The key is to be able to get a career where you make enough money to pay a significant amount in taxes, then get a "trade or business" to offset some of those taxes. Then you have a greater chance of getting money back from the taxes you have paid in and making money at the trade or business.

Money can be a motivator for some and a de-motivator for others. It is important to keep your finances under control so you are not a slave to your financial choices.

Networking

Networking is making contact with people and remembering them. Networking is remembering teachers, coaches, political people, administrators, etc. At some point in time, you may need others to write a letter of recommendation for you. Remember, in order to have other people assist you, you must assist other people. There may be an opportunity to help others when networking. It is important to understand that when we help others, we should do it because it is the "right thing to do" and NOT to keep track and expect people to "OWE you one." Networking is surrounding yourself with people who you can help and who can help you in the future. Make an evolving list of names, phone numbers, interests, etc. of the people you meet. Keep it current. This will help you tremendously in the years to come.

Partnering

In order to reach our goals, we may need the help of other people. This is called partnering. Partnering is recruiting the help of other people to assist us in achieving our goals and dreams. Athletics involves a lot of partnering. You may partner with a coach to master your offense or defense. He may partner with a camp to develop your skills. He may partner with your strengthening / conditioning coach to increase your speed or your strength. You may partner with a teacher to maintain your grades. There are many areas in life that we consciously or unconsciously partner with others to assist us in achievement.

If you find an area or establish a goal that you may need help with, it is important to ask for the assistance of others. Many times people will freely and graciously help you to achieve your goals. None of us have all the answers. It is important to partner with people who may have those answers. Use the knowledge of others to help you achieve your goals. We partner with others in many areas of our lives, from going to the grocery store for weekly shopping, to hiring accountants and attorneys to put complicated business deals together. Many people are hesitant to ask others for help, but in reality, we are all dependent on others to achieve our goals. Most people are willing to help—just ask. Remember to get partners and be a partner. You can have everything in life you want, if you are willing to help enough people get what they want. Once you think you know it all, you do not. Smart people learned from their experiences. Wise people learn from the experiences of others. There are many people waiting to help you. All you have to do is ask.

Basics of Athletics

Weight training:

Develop strength with high weight and low reps (one- to three-reps sets)

Develop tone with low weight and high reps (eight- to twelve-rep sets)

Full-body activities are best for general health and athletics (squat, dead lifts, power cleans, etc)

Foot speed:

There are four components that all need to be trained to develop sprint speed.

1. Stride length
2. Stride frequency
3. Speed endurance
4. Running form

Agility training:

There are four components of agility training.

1. Acceleration
2. Deceleration

3. Changing of direction (core body strength)
4. Acceleration (again)

Explosive power training:

This is training at your maximum speed for the weight you are lifting (medicine balls, explosive push ups, depth jumps, etc.).

Flexibility training:

This is training that increases flexibility. This is important because flexibility decreases the chance of injury, increases a muscle length, and allows you more free range of movement.

Coordination and balance:

This is training that helps your body understand where all its parts are in space. The medical term for this is called "proprioception." This allows better control of your body and quicker reaction time. Remember, a tenth of a second can mean the difference between the touchdown and a tackle in the backfield.

Understanding Time

It is important as a young person that you understand time. Every day you have an opportunity to advance yourself in one way or another. Every day you have an opportunity to make yourself better or make yourself worse. Understand that you do not stay the same. The momentum of change does not sit still for very long. You are either moving up the ladder, or you are falling down a ladder. Many older people look back at their life and wish they would have done some things differently.

For example, the twenty-five-year-old cannot play high school football any longer. That time has passed. It is lost forever. This holds true for many different activities. Give yourself the opportunity to have exposure to many different areas. Then choose what you feel you will have the most success in. Remember, no hard work is ever wasted. Hard work today will help you for tomorrow. Hard work today will prepare you for the opportunities of tomorrow, if you are able to recognize them. If you see an opportunity and don't take advantage of that opportunity, then that time is gone. It is important to understand the concept of time. It is important to value time and not waste it. If you don't think a minute is important, ask a parent who has lost a child in a store and then finds them. If you don't think a second is important, hold your head under water for as long as he can. If you don't think a hundredth of a second is important, ask the second-place finisher in the Olympic hundred-meter dash. Time is something to understand, cherish, and respect. You can waste your money and you can waste your things, but don't waste your time because your time is a part of your life. Wasted time is a wasted life. Choose how you spend your time wisely.

Understanding Time Management

Time is a continuous period measured by clocks, watches, and calendars. Time is one of the most precious resources we have. Time is also one of the most misunderstood, misused, and mismanaged resources. A person can replace material items or money, but a person cannot replace time. No matter how many things you acquire or how much money you attain, you can never replace the time you've spent. Once time is spent, it is gone forever. It is extremely important to understand time, so you will know how to spend it wisely. The following are some ways to evaluate how to manage your time.

The four common situations on how time is spent:

Situation 1: urgent and important. You perceive most situations as urgent and important, forcing you to immediately react to them. If you find yourself in this situation often, you may become very stressed and unable to fulfill the needs of everyday life. This puts other people in control of your time and puts added stress into your life. Many people suffer from panic attacks, anxiety, and other health problems from being in this situation.

Situation 2: Not urgent, but important. You perceive most situations as important, but not urgent, allowing you to prioritize them and react when you feel it is necessary. This is a situation that you want to be in most of your life. It allows you to pick and choose your issues and what you are going to do to resolve the issues. This gives you control of your time and your life.

Situation 3: Urgent, but not important. You perceive situations as urgent but chose not to respond. This is the person who knows he has a test the next day, knows he has to study for the test, but chooses not to study. This person is perceived as lazy.

Situation 4: Not urgent and not important. You perceive situations as not urgent and not important. This type of person sits in front of the TV, computer, or videogame all day and gets very little accomplished. This person has very low stress and accomplishes very little in life.

It is important for us to understand that the use of time is a choice. All of us will use all four of these situations at one time or another. If you find yourself in situations 1, 3, or 4 you'll have less productivity with the time you have available. If you find yourself in situation 2 most of the time, you'll have the best control of your time, the least amount of stress in your life, and the maximum amount of productivity. Your time is under your control. Keep yourself in situation 2. Everyone has twenty-four hours a day and seven days a week. How you choose to manage your time will impact your level of success.

Understanding the "Cycles of Life"

As we go through life we find ourselves fluctuating from the bottom of our game, working our way to the top, and then starting over again. This is what I call the "Cycles of Life."

A good example of this is in our school system. When we enter our middle school system in the sixth grade, we are given more opportunities than what we had in the elementary school. More opportunities develop more responsibilities. More responsibilities develop more growth. More growth develops the ability to expand your life, if you choose.

For example, in middle school (sixth through eighth grade) a person may be involved in athletics. Many times students all practice together. There are many times two groups of players: a first-string (varsity), and a second-string (junior varsity). As a sixth-grader you generally come into the program on the second string (junior varsity) and "work your way up" to the first string (varsity) over the next few weeks or years. Understand that you enter this program as a "low man" and gradually prove your ability, working your way up through the program.

This same process will happen to you many times in life. This process occurs again as you start your ninth-grade (freshman) year of high school and continues until you graduate from high school your twelfth-grade year, as a senior. This same process occurs again if you go to college (freshman through senior). This process occurs again if you go to postgraduate school or find your first job. This process happens again when you change your job/career or receive a promotion. This is what I call the "Cycles of Life." You start out everything you do as the "low man" and have an opportunity to "prove yourself." When you are "proving yourself," your superiors are not only looking at your knowledge. Your superiors are also looking at your "life skills." Many people may have the knowledge to do your job, but many do not have the "life skills" to do that job well. These "life skills" are many; your decision making, your ability to communicate, your ability to listen, your ability to apply the needs of the organization, your attitude, your honesty, your integrity, your perseverance, your self-control, your leadership skills, etc. Knowledge and applying "life skills" will increase your success rate and will keep you on top of your game.

Understanding the "Cycles of Life" will help you understand that you will start at the bottom. You will advance by proving yourself and your ability. If you expect to advance, your superiors/customers will expect you to work and work hard to prove to them that you are deserving of advancement.

Understanding the "Cycles of Life" will assist you in understanding where you are in your schooling/job/career and assist you in evaluating yourself and what is expected of you to advance.

Understanding Friends and Acquaintances

Having friends and acquaintances is good as long as you are in control of your decision-making. When teaching this program to high school students, I like to use the following example. Everyone sit up and look around. Take a good look at everyone around you. Take a look at your close friends, your not-so-close friends, the people you respect, and the people you have little respect for. Understand this: You freshmen, in four years you will never see most of these people again. You sophomores, in three years you will never see most of these people again. You juniors, in two years you will never see most of these people again. You seniors, in less than one year, you will never see most of these people again. So when developing your life, why would you care what they think? Why would you let any one of these people influence your decisions? You know what is right and what is wrong. Why would you let any of them "talk you into" doing something that is wrong? Why would you listen to them if they tell you your idea/goal/dream is stupid or unworthy? After high school, you will not see them again to celebrate your success or learn from your failure.

This same process will go on again and again in life. As you go through college, get a job, get a new job, move to a different town, etc., your friends and acquaintances will change. In the future, you will randomly cross paths with your friends and acquaintances just like "weaves in a web." Remember, you choose your own life. You choose your own direction. It is important to listen to the opinions of friends and family, but understand that your choices will control your destiny.

Understanding Problems

A problem is a situation that is difficult to deal with or where it is difficult to decide the best course of action. We all have problems. Some problems may be bigger or smaller than others. Some people dwell on their problems and consistently talk about problems. Some people cannot get past their problems. Quite frankly, people do not care about our problems, and most people do not want to hear about our problems. Most people are willing to listen to another person's problems out of respect but can do little to help the situation. If you are fortunate enough to have a close friend or relative, they can help you talk through your problems and come up with a solution for you to address and learn from. It is important to understand that problems need to be addressed and learned from, but not focused on. It is important to look at opportunities and positive experiences more than dwelling on problems. If we dwell on problems, we will get more problems. If we focus on opportunities and positive experiences, we will get more opportunities and positive experiences. The choice is yours.

The Basics of Religion

Please do not be offended by this section. I removed this section from this book two separate times and knew it was the wrong approach. Please take this for what it is worth and apply anything that you can or just skip over it. It was important to me that I kept it in.

Understand that there are many forms of religion: Catholic, Lutheran, United Church of Christ, Methodist, Buddhism, Jehovah Witness, and others. I want you to understand some basics of religion. In college and in life you will be exposed to many forms of religion. Traditional forms of religion include going to church, reading the Bible, etc., and there are fringe forms of religion with people preaching on street corners. There is no right or wrong, although some forms of religion are more acceptable to the general public than others. Be careful of the fringe forms of religion. These are the ones that can challenge your thoughts, causing you to second-guess the way you were raised and question your faith. Understand that to be "born again" is to decide that you believe in God. When you are born through your mother, that is a physical birth. To be "born again" is a spiritual birth. Some people have never been exposed to a "higher power." In my case we chose God. In our family, our children grew up with God in their life. We feel they were lucky. Remember, there are many belief systems about religion. In our belief system, Jesus Christ has died for all of our sins. Understand that God is always with you. When you make a mistake, ask for God's forgiveness and move on. God forgives *all* sins, no matter how big or small. Believe in Jesus Christ, believe in God, and know they are always there to guide you. All you have to do is pray to them, ask for their help or forgiveness, and read the Bible to see how you are to live. Remember to be thankful for all of God's gifts. Church is an excellent way to understand the higher powers above, but it is not the only way.

If you choose to read the bible,

please read and remember: John 3:16
                             Matthew 22:37–40
                             Matthew 11: 28–30

Read "Proverbs," the entire chapter, over and over again. This section tells you how to live your life and run a business.

> Happy moments—praise God.
> Difficult moments—seek God.
> Quiet moments—worship God.
> Painful moments—trust in God.
> Every moment—thank God.

For those who respect another "higher power" besides a god, good for you; apply the principals above. For those who do not respect a "higher power," that is your choice, just as respecting God is ours. There is no right or wrong.

People vs. Things

Understand that "people" are more important than "things." "Things" such as a new car, a new home, a four-wheeler, or money do not bring you happiness. Have as much or more respect for the people who care about you than the "things" you have. Care about the "people" who are important to you. Care about family, good friends, relatives, etc. The things that you receive are much less important than the relationships you build. "People" are more important than "things."

You Only Have Control of Yourself

Some people think they can help or change others. People can only be helped or changed if they want to be helped or changed. It is important to understand that you only have control of yourself. You have control of how you think, act, and react to the people and things around you.

For some reason it is quite easy to recognize the weaknesses of the people you're closest to. Many times, this may be a friend, family member, spouse/girlfriend, brother/sister, child, classmate, etc. Please remember, if you want others to recognize the good in you—recognize the good in others. If you choose to be critical of others—others will be critical of you.

Many people feel pointing out the faults of others helps them in some way. This is truly "stinkin' thinkin'." The people who think that way will be "stinkin'," as will the people around them who "buy into" this philosophy.

Below is a list of "life traits" that develop "relationship suicide."

1. Choosing to recognize and point out the weaknesses/faults of others.
2. Choosing to say "I told you so" when the other has made a mistake.
3. Choosing to argue with others.
4. Choosing to "boss" others around.
5. Choosing to use negative consequence techniques. Example: If you do not… I will not…
6. Choosing to be demeaning and/or belittling.
7. Choosing to use others as an excuse for your failures. Example: It was because of you I can't…
8. Choosing to hold a grudge.
9. Choosing to think "lack" and giving up.

These are the symptoms of what I call the "tornado of a failing relationship." Sometimes stopping a tornado would be easier than stopping this way of choosing to interact in a relationship. As you can see, these are all choices. The way we look at others is something we can all change. Your perception is your reality. Not everything in the world is horrible. There is an equal amount of good as there is bad. If you want "more bad," focus on the "bad." If you want "more good," focus on the "good."

If you want good relationships with your friends, family, spouse, children, and others, it is best to make the following choices:

1. Choose to recognize and point out the strengths of others.
2. Choose to not say, "I told you so." Give support to others and help them through their failed choices.
3. Choose to not argue; choose to use helpful questioning.
4. Choose to not "boss" others. Help them to evaluate the pros and cons of their situation and let them choose.
5. Choose to not use negative consequence techniques. Choose to love and give of yourself and your time unconditionally. Do not "keep track" and think that another person "owes you one." Trust that they will make the right choices. Make sure to

recognize when they do make the right choice and tell them. When they do not make the right choices, help them learn from their mistakes.

6. Choose to not demean or belittle. Choose to encourage and assist others in developing their goals and dreams.

7. Choose to not use others as excuses for your mistakes/failures. Choose to take 100 percent responsibility for your actions and reactions. "If it is going to be, it's up to me." Take responsibility for your successes and your successful failures.

8. Choose to not hold a grudge. Holding a grudge will hold you back like an anchor on a ship.

9. Choose to not think "lack"; think "abundance." Choose to not "give up"; choose perseverance. Celebrate your success and evaluate your successful failures.

10. Choose to care.

11. Choose to compliment.

12. Choose to encourage.

13. Choose to recognize the good in all things and tell the world.

14. Choose to be an active listener.

15. Choose to be nonjudgmental.

16. Choose to support others.

17. Choose to see what *you* can do or change about *you* to make your life better.

These are some of the ways you can *"choose"* to have great relationships with others. You cannot change what others think, say, or do. You only have control of yourself. How you think, communicate, and interact with others will determine your destiny. You only have control of yourself.

Have Fun

Have fun in life. Having fun breeds happiness. Have fun in your career, with your family, with learning, with exercise, with training, with your job, etc.—have fun with all you do in life. Having fun allows you and the people around you to enjoy life. Enjoying life is the key to happiness.

Be Happy

Happiness is the ability to express pleasure or good. Happiness is the ability to be pleased with something and express that pleasure with internal feelings of gratitude, or communicate that pleasure with a facial expression, verbally, with body language, etc. Happiness is generally created by looking at the good or positive in the world around us. Some people are unable to look at the good and only see the bad or negative. These people are generally perceived as negative or unhappy. Happiness is the choice of looking at the good around us and communicating it to others. One happy person can light up a room. Happiness is how we think, not what we have or what we become. Happiness is contagious; unfortunately, so is the lack of it. People are as happy as they choose to be.

Purpose in Life

Live life by your morals, ethics, and core values. Be willing to help people who "want" to be helped, not "need" to be helped.

Our purpose for life on earth is to enrich our life and the lives of others.

Please keep this book in a convenient place where you will be able to reference it in the future when/if you are struggling or just need it for review. I wish I had something like this when I was growing up. If you follow these concepts, you will be much farther ahead than anyone around you.

Please use the information in this book to bring out the best in you and your family and enhance the lives of those around you. If you choose to help others, please consider using this book's partner book, titled *Developing Mental Toughness—Teaching the Game of Life*.

Please apply the information in this book. Get excited about you and your future! You need to accept the fact that from this moment on, your future is in capable hands—YOURS!

Thank you for spending your time reading this book.

Together we can change the world by recognizing one positive experience at a time.

About the Author

Dr. Timothy S. Wakefield is married and a father of three boys. He is a Doctor of Chiropractic, Diplomate in the American Chiropractic Board of Sports Physicians, Certified Strength and Conditioning Specialist and Certified in Chiropractic Spinal Trauma. He has published books, articles and taught multiple programs in the area of sports injuries, physical fitness, health wellness, occupational health, athletic development, motivation, etc.

Dr. Wakefield is a firm believer that the "mental game of life" is "teachable and learnable". Before a person can teach the game of life a person must understand the game of life. To implement these life skills it is Dr. Wakefield's opinion that people must be mentally strong to reject the distractions that impede our success. Thus the name of the book: *Mental Toughness – Understanding the Game of Life*.